Sinéad M⟨...⟩ Her awards
include ⟨...⟩ ⟨Liter⟩ary Fellowship,
first prize in t⟨...⟩ion, the Irish Times
Poetry Prize (2009, 2013), and the T. S. Eliot Prize (2013). *Parallax
and Selected Poems* (Farrar Straus & Giroux) was shortlisted for the
National Book Critics' Circle Award for Poetry in 2015 and in 2016
she received the E. M. Forster Award from the American Academy
of Arts and Letters. In 2017 *On Balan⟨...⟩* ⟨P⟩rize for
Best Colle⟨...⟩ ⟨...⟩ral Poet
Laureate and is currently Professor of Creative Writing at Newcastle
University.

ON THE COVER: Al-Jazari, 'a Peacock Basin', from the *Book of Knowledge
of Ingenious Mechanical Devices* (1206).

ON
BALANCE

Sinéad Morrissey

CARCANET

First published in Great Britain in 2017 by
CARCANET PRESS LTD
Alliance House, 30 Cross Street
Manchester M2 7AQ
www.carcanet.co.uk

A CIP catalogue record for this book is available
from the British Library: ISBN 9781784103606.

Book design: Luke Allan.
Printed and bound in England by SRP Ltd.

The publisher acknowledges financial assistance
from Arts Council England.

CONTENTS

for my three parents

By the cables
　　　　　of electric strands,
I recognize
　　　　the era succeeding
　　　　　　　　the steam age –
here
　　men
　　　　had ranted
　　　　　　on radio.
Here
　　men
　　　　had ascended
　　　　　　　in planes.

VLADIMIR MAYAKOVSKY, 'Brooklyn Bridge' (1925)
translated by Max Hayward and George Reavey

It never looks warm or properly daytime
in black-and-white photographs the sheer cliff-
face of the ship still enveloped in its scaffolding
backside against the launching cradle
ladies lining the quay in their layered drapery
touching their gloves to their lips and just as
They That Go Down to the Sea in Ships rises
from choirboys' mouths in wisps and snatches
and evil skitters off and looks askance
for now a switch is flicked at a distance
and the moment swollen with catgut-
about-to-snap with ice picks hawks' wings
pine needles eggshells bursts and it starts
grandstand of iron palace of rivets starts
moving starts slippery-sliding down
slow as a snail at first in its viscous passage
taking on slither and speed gathering in
the Atlas-capable weight of its own momentum
tonnage of grease beneath to get it waterborne
tallow soft soap train oil a rendered whale
this last the only Millihelen her beauty
slathered all over the slipway
faster than a boy with a ticket in his pocket
might run alongside it the bright sheet
of the Lough advancing faster than a tram
heavy chains and anchors kicking in
lest it outdoes itself straining up
to a riot of squeals and sparks lest it capsizes
before its beginning lest it drenches
the aldermen and the ship sits back in the sea
as though it were ordinary and wobbles
ever so slightly and then it and the sun-splashed
titled hills the railings the pin-striped awning
in fact everything regains its equilibrium.

Processions that lack high stilts have nothing that catches the eye
and yes, by three hours in we're jaded, frankly. The baby
tiger, stupid with drugs, we fondled and got flashed with
has been taken away by the scruff of his silver chain and the woman
undressing and dressing herself again inside a fire-filled hoop
without a single glimmer of skin is running out
of costumes. How this cacophonous spectaculum will finish
is anybody's guess: our kids are so bored and sugared up
they're about to froth with tears, like soda fountains.

                                              Mozart's 25TH.
Acrobats in wigs in lace in *Amadeus* cuffs file into place
as the audience coughs, then quiets.   One by one they jackknife

onto a trampoline and using their dear launched breakable
selves as pens, as flares, sketch out for us in air what isn't there:
a simple x, then denser, higher – cat's-cradle architecture
strung taut as piano wire, rigging, fountains, the winged
horse in the sky, all his star points joined together, and as
they angle backwards to land like so many stackable chairs
on their comrades' shoulders, it's not just the absence
of gravity we'll remember – bodies being impossible –
but the way we imagined we could reach out and touch
the co-ordinates of the Battle of Stalingrad.

ON BALANCE

May you be ordinary;
Have, like other women,
An average of talents:
Not ugly, not good-looking,
Nothing uncustomary
To pull you off your balance [...]
In fact, may you be dull

PHILIP LARKIN, 'BORN YESTERDAY'

Even fully grown,
she'd be a 'girl' to you.
You rarely mention women,
except to stress our looks
or what we cannot do,
though 'girls' persist
in separate, lit-up boxes –
their pants pulled down,
or getting fucked
by your luckier friend
in the toilet of a train.

You were the mean fairy
at the christening,
feigning honesty.
No doubt her father slapped
you on the back,
admired your dazzling
final turn from lack
to grudging benediction.
I wouldn't let you near
my brilliant daughter –
so far, in fact, from *dull*,
that *radiant, incandescent*
are as shadows on the landscape
after staring at the sun.

RECEIVING THE DEAD

for Jimmy McAleavey

1

Elementary, Watson,
        that the dead are legion,
eager to speak & awaiting
        a Wireless Telegraph
System to usher them in;
        that the pain of aeons
is galvanising… Bats chittering
        inside a cave's auditorium
or a thousand starlings
        amplifying evening over
the sodden docks: that sounds
        like this might issue forth
as soon as he flicks the switch
        should not be shocking –
receiver without transmitter,
        plugging itself into
the disturbed nest of the afterworld
        where everyone's still
at home, this amber lacquered box
        contains within its frame
the fits & shredded ectoplasm
        of our own dear century
in a twentieth-century form & bids
        all the dead welcome.
Listen –

2

A choir of fire –
      you are being watched
my little Friedel – the door jamb
      jammed & undulating,
the discarnate jostling for position
      at the microphone –
tell Daddy I'm – *the key's in your blue*
      coat pocket – *Selah* –
can't you remember? – giggles
      ascending their scales
then stopping, weeping, warnings –
      a war is – singing –
All She Gets from the Ice Man is Ice
      – whingeing –
you fucking knew I never meant to –
      Christ – diaphanous
acoustic entry point clogged
      & venomous, or worse,
tedious – *rain followed by snow* –
      let downs & come ons –
a baby who can't yet speak unleashing
      a caterwaul – instructions –
overhaul – *I'm sorry* not nearly as often
      as you'd think
& *believe me* more often.

3

To picture them, Watson,
        the only way we know how:
as Lazarus, say, pitched up
        on the other side for the second
time, in the coat of his own
        rot, but human, or the worst
of them pinned to their isolate
        stations, islands in a lake,
sheeted white & penancing,
        then hearing the click,
the chink made actual, the beckoning,
        to see them come running,
the boys & girls & men & women,
        their bare feet flashing –
is to err extravagantly. It must be.
        In the distances between
Signal Hill & Rathlin, between
        the curved horizon of Earth
& the ionosphere, they have become
        pure air, pure interruption –
a disturbance like a storm, further
        down the line, undressed
by electromagnetism. But wholly
        literate, they are equivalent
to language in its given state.

The two of us wound
into borrowed kimonos
on the temple steps

I see our future
daughter driving a ragtop
and then I wake or

my heavy headgear
dagger tucked into my waist-
band should you ever

don't and there's this trick
your skin still does if I brush
my thumb along it

undress another
one flick of my ivory
wrist and I'd collapse

thronged notes spun into
one held hum by a gesture
all the hares lie down

in the wet of my
small intestine my stomach
bridles soon enough

and the two of us
just under half our lives and
this glitch we ride in

over uncooked eggs
at the airport and you you
star you crucible

space together I
see precisely no one else
inside a shrinking

my teeth are yours I
think my ribs removable
your unwavering

bubble of light the
minuscule part of matter
that's matter splitting

lantern frown above
my ice bed bloody sheets your
trousseau in my dream

apart from itself
bright you singing on the stair-
way there's only you

The assembly hall is full, though it's early still:
mums and dads on loan from their workaday offices;
littler brothers and sisters crashed out in pushchairs
and parked along the aisle like outsize baggage.
Chat rises up to perch among the rafters
and gets steadily amplified, making the walls resound.
Stewed tea in too-thin plastic scalds our hands.

And then it's dark and started. The Principal stands,
reminds us of the exits. He occupies his moment
so deliberately he might be chairing Congress.
And a decree went out. And all the boys and girls.
That all the world and several weeks' rehearsals
should be taxed. And thanks to those who helped
with sewing and thanks to those who witnessed

in their houses that a child was born this day
and thanks to everyone for turning up and time
to welcome the fixed astonishing star over Bethlehem
and all the other stars and please applause.
We turn as heliotropes to the sun to watch
a hundred preternaturally tiny children follow
their teachers in, and almost fail to recognise

our sons and daughters amongst them, so cleanly
have they been lifted from their context, so
splendidly have they been managing without us.
The chorus is dressed in red and green, the animals
in animal costumes, ten of them wear wings,
and here come the key anointed individuals –
the Virgin, the Husband, the Keeper, the Soldier –

they of transitive voices, survivors of many tests,
like Odysseus, whose reward is a human name
and, bar the two dear faces in the distance, backlit
with adoration, a room of strangers staring at them.
Narrators rise and fall to call the action points.
The songs break in as ponderous punctuation
and are exhausting for everyone. We half expect

the children to unhook themselves
from the strings of their teachers' attention
and to cry, or laugh, to scatter like birds off a lake,
but they don't, not now, not yet, and we are left
with a row of just-licked-by-a-cow-looking boys
in dressing gowns, Mary in a dress, Immanuel
in his cradle, low-key and ineffable, a portent

pointing the star of herself in two directions
at once, and this studded arena we've led them to,
these people whom we've forged, whose frankincense
we breathed when they were born, and we're sorry,
but we don't know how it happened, or what
the instructions are – we've left them in itchy
kneesocks, holding up a sign – or how it will end.

Craigavon, 1977

A girl is drowning.
      A cuckoo is throwing
its voice in the trees
      to the back of us
and we are eating my mother's
      wholemeal-bread
sandwiches on an overhang
      after our swim.
The girl is the tallest girl in my class
      and I have never
known her name. In the dark
      of my granny's room
at home there's a map
      of Ireland on the wall
made from Guinness glasses.
      Her fine blonde hair
keeps surfacing like pond weed
      and then her forehead
but she can't get her mouth
      up high enough
out of the water to scream.
      As she falls
she's a milk bottle plunged
      under in the sink
though her whiteness will not
      rinse clean. *Oh Dougal,*
say her air bubbles, *Oh Zebedee.*
      The ghosts in the grave-
yard by Kilwilkie Estate
      are waving at a train.
The girl is bouncing
      on an underwater
trampoline but slowing down.

The girl I was
last winter has hung up
        her snot-covered
poncho on a digger bucket
        (hundreds of tonnes
of sand to build a beach!)
        and can do breaststroke.
I think I must nudge my father
        who is brown and skinny
and thirty and whose shirt
        is a flash on the grass,
suddenly. And when the long
        and dripping shine
of her sleeping body is laid
        alongside us there is
not a mark on her. Losses so far:
        the tank of my brother's
frogspawn in the garden frozen
        as thick as a phone book;
our neighbour driven off
        in an ambulance who
never came back; my skipping-
        rope. Then she vomits
what she's swallowed right there
        beside the oranges
and the crisp packets and the
        lay-me-down
servants in waiting stand up
        and walk.

PERFUME

1

23 May 1963

My Great Auntie Winnie may as well have spotted a crack
        in the floor of Nottingham's Odeon Cinema –
                beginning under the stage
like a telltale hairline fissure in a dam face
        then zigzagging towards the exit –
                as have been struck
by the actual bellwether that assailed her
        the morning she trudged in to sweep and mop
                and dust the flip-back seats
after the pop music concert the night before:
        not just the common-enough stench of smoke
                and sweat, but an extra still-warm
acrid musk, the mixed-in fug of a stable
        in summer heat, hitting her like the reek
                of a hospital laundry,
because in answer to *Love Me Do*, offered up
        in spectacular harmony, two hundred
                fourteen-year-old girls
had instantly wet themselves, screaming *Yes!*
        We love you already!, but inaudibly,
                each lone voice hopeless
against the squealing sheetmetal square of noise,
        and so their bodies had taken over,
                take this river, each shower a gift,
intimate and articulate, to whichever identikit member
        they'd pinned their collapsing
                stomachs on, each stream of steaming
yellow a flower, and as the crack grew ever wider
        and plaster flakes abandoned the ceiling
                and covered my Auntie's rollered

hair, she suddenly saw the street outside
divide the length of the fissure, then the city,
the north, the south, then all of England,
mothers on one side, daughters on the other,
and the chasm between them strung
with brilliant washing –
socks and vests and stockings and skirts and pants,
rinsed clean with a bluebag in the kitchen sink,
lifting in the wind.

12 February 1964

Picture it again
rope-throated by the scaffold
of scent so exquisite
to save him
their grannies serving them tea
Grew weirder
stacked along corridors
as if their children were scrofulous
or Jesus
had to stay so in tune
like slipping their arms
or balancing
They shredded
They auctioned off
Fans showed up
chambermaid uniforms
their car would be crawling
within seconds
shrieking to get
For all his dastardly
he went too far
on his wafted handkerchief
and so they unslippered him
out of love
They had to steal
like miscreants
bundled into
or fish vans
the boys they were
the Liverpool Lads
waving wildly
over

the hero at the end
unstoppers a bottle
the crowd pours round
It was weird from the beginning
on a saucer
Crutches & drips
mothers begging their touch
& they were Royalty Restored
They couldn't hear a thing
with one another
inside somebody else's sleeves
blindfolded
their hotel sheets
their knives & forks
in commandeered
If they left by the wrong exit
with women
faces of owls at the windscreen
let in
ravishment
whatever it was he unleashed
too much to bear
out of his skin
& ate him
from those seething stadiums
from a crime scene
laundry trucks
They left behind
as decoys
who cried to be famous
in the other direction
here

It takes ten thousand hours to shine at anything.
And if we haven't spent night after night on the Reeperbahn

cranking our act so tight it stood up all by itself and walked,
we've come close, but we still fall flat.

We sweat inside our Sullivan suits. The early set is hell:
each song like a crackerjack firework, jettisoning its effects

inside its white-hot flurry of minutes then cutting out.
We can hear the gap – by a bit, by a notch, by a semi-step,

by a skip in the heart we can't fix – no matter the hours
the prayers the floral tributes the slow dispensing of oil

at its feet. It's a rainy January night in Belfast.
I need to tell my son when I see him about the lights

of another ferry across from ours on the journey over
like we were two boats holding hands.

1

Though he never once placed a bet, my grandfather
sat in his chair every day and picked out winners:
Larkspur, League of Nations, Isinglass, Never Say Die

in the 2:30 at Epsom or Newmarket.
He'd follow their dips and peaks, ingesting the painfully
difficult newsprint on off-work afternoons,

or he'd rely on the tug-at-his-sleeve of instinct:
his grandmother's Romani nous with horses, his blacksmith-
father's apprising sense bred into his muscles and veins...

And so his damaged house filled up with winnings:
tickets to a race, pairs of boots to choose from,
a tea cosy from a shop, a pigeon cote out the back,

and after each spectacular nose-across-the-finish-line
outsider made him rich (which happened twice)
he'd sit and eat his wedding supper over again in his imagined

life: ham on the bone; salmon, roast beef, egg-and-cress; a cake.

2

No matter the shift, the only food he'd take with him
down the pit was bread and jam, two slices wrapped up
in greaseproof paper, and a bottle of gone-cold tea.

He'd perch in a cranny to eat it halfway through
his eight-hour stint at the coalface, black as a bat
bar the whites and reds of his eyes and his teeth's gapped ivory.

Each mine an auditorium. Under the fallen sun
of his headlamp, like the ghost of the boy he was
at the sorting station sorting out nuts from brights,

he'd array the sounds the tunnels carried
– the squeal of the wheel, an invisible neighbour's cough –
discarding each in turn until, in his blue-scarred palm,

he held up gold: miners' saviours in cages singing their lack
half a mile off, back by the fluted shaft, singing
no black damp, no gas, until he'd sing himself.

He knew eight-and-twenty ways to raise the roof, some safe, most not.

What possessed my granny, slim, smart, solvent, raising the roof
every Friday night after work at the Palais de Danse
in Nottingham, showing the band what-for with spies and soldiers,

to marry him? Some runaway freight car undid her, shunting her north.
Already his breath was a wounded animal pacing its ever-decreasing
circle underneath his rib cage. He couldn't afford linoleum.

The village had five shops. He was born in the reign of Victoria;
they'd finally buried the dead of Ypres just as my granny
came caterwauling in. Once, as a child,

visiting her spinster-aunt's friend in the countryside
who kept house for her younger brother, she was privy to this:
a walking shadow, the size and shape of a man,

stole across the room towards the kitchen, not touching anything.
The kettle's whistle. Splashing. Singing. Then the shut door
opened abruptly and out stepped a white vest and a clean face

and the moon's penumbra vanished into brightness.

4

Bright as a whitebell in Handley Wood, bright as the heads
of poor man's pepper shaking their throwaway lace
all over the lanes between New Whit and Eckington

was the evening he proposed (and the proud hart fleet
upon the enclosing hills and the honeycomb oozing honey).
And late the next day he stepped into a cage

and fell the length of a tarpitch mile, not looking, *yes,*
to where pit ponies stamped in their stalls, not listening, *yes,*
and was out along a by-line

dreaming his Skegness honeymoon into place
when a heaped tub of altogether coal, *yes you Tom Goodwin,*
yes, began snarling his name.

You might measure the force of its freak uncoupling
by what was crushed: it took an hour to manage the mess
of lungs and bones and blood to the surface.

He sat out in blankets and looked at the sea for his month at the
                                        Miners' Rest.

A month at a Miners' Rest, alright, but no compensation –
every time she paid a coal bill, or dressed my mother
in a cousin's pinafore, my granny would preen and peck

at the elderly man grown elderly early
hunched across from her in his armchair.
He'd turn himself into a tree and wouldn't answer.

And the silence of Glasshouse Lane burred with thistledown
like a blanket sewn by swallows just for them
would settle over the room

and he'd light up a woodbine and smile until she smiled too
and then the damp-blotched ceiling would open
and in their last companionable hours together

they'd play host to strange familiar visitors
soft-landing expertly in amongst the furniture:
Eric Coates *Calling All Workers*; Ralph Elman and his Bohemian
                                                            Players;

Ron and Ethel taking forever to get nowhere in *Take It from Here*.

6

Because the distances you travel are unimaginable
to the man who flicks open each wing in a fan-card flourish
checking for balance and corkiness

before shunting you onto the train for your journey south
and over the freezing sea
towards liberation at Rheims or Poitiers

and because your tiny friable arrangement of magnets and air pockets
through which the planet articulates its cleverness
might be crushed by a falcon in an instant, but isn't,

and because your most exhilarating trajectory
is not just from darkness to light, as his is,
but from darkness to the upper storeys of the air itself –

coaxing you down off the toss from Bordeaux or Nantes
to the landing board, getting your leg-ring clocked,
is to stand with a capful of coins in the Miners' Arms, a balloon
                                                    adventurer,

or like a man who has tasted the rind of the moon, without ever
                                                    leaving home.

MY SEVENTEENTH-CENTURY GIRLHOOD

(after a title by Gillian Allnut)

Because the Dear Lord God is both in me
& in His Book, my father said,
these two must cross. He tasked me daily,

under the lantern clock, each white-
clothed afternoon, with heavy words.
Which I would guess.

Firmament. Sixth.
Then, in a rush, the *Book of Martyrs*
sprang to life & flashed, as by itself,

& all I did was watch.

～

Mother borrowed me back
for bedsheets & fires & batch loaves & babies' napkins
– in Summer the shucking –

& Mr Thomas Davers, who soon came calling.
His hat. His manners.
I was fourteen years old & already bleeding.

My Aunts walked up for the wedding.

～

The days had no more avenues
to read or wander in. Soon enough
another baby girl unclenched her fist

& the boy born dead stared up
at me out of the cauldron
when I washed our Sunday best.

To *Sepulchre*, *Commandment*
(all mine are thine & thine are mine)
I added new words of my own:

Countess Cakes at Christmastime. Dragonfly. Machine.

THE MAYFLY

i.m. Lilian Bland, 1878–1971

Conspicuously mis-christened – what chink
  in the general atmosphere, what sudden
    lift of bones and breath

      allowed you to stand up straight in mechanic's overalls
        (*skirts are out of the question*) and plot
          your escape route into the sky?

          Like the right foot of Louis Blériot,
            trapped beside one of his overheating
              engines, like the umpteen previous

biplane extravaganzas that had left the ground
  – *gadzooks!* – for a couple of minutes
    only to wobble uncontrollably

      in recalcitrant space and then nosedive,
        everything flared white hot
          for you until it abruptly ended:

          jujutsu, shooting, horseracing,
            spending days on remote Scottish
              islands photographing seabirds.

You donned your Donegal cap
  (*the natives, I hear, thought one of the mills
    had blown up but put it down*

      to a thunderstorm) and tapped your cigarette ash
        all over Edwardian decorum;
          if Blériot wouldn't let you near

his Channel-hopping aeroplane –
you'd begged him in a letter
to crown you as his passenger –

you'd build and fly your own.
The unflexed, held-aloft wingspan
of gulls in flight was where you started,

in the Tobercorran workshop,
your gardener's-son assistant
holding your tools and worshipping

you from a distance. *I enclose
two photos of my biplane,
the 'Mayfly'; she is the first*

biplane to be made in Ireland:
skids of ash, ribs and stanchions
of spruce, bamboo outriggers

taut beneath unbleached calico,
more grasshopper than aircraft.
You ran the finished may-fly,

may-not fly still missing its engine
and airy as a climbing frame off the top
of Carnmoney Hill,

Belfast smouldering under its furnaces,
the Lough a phlegmatic eye,
casually watching, and hung

as a counterweight four six-foot
volunteers from the Irish Constabulary
who saw the ground ripped clear

of their feet in an upward gust
and were trailed alarmingly over
heads of astonished livestock

before dropping off.
In the movie of your life
they haven't scripted yet

all bets are on from this moment
(*it is quite a new sensation being charged
by an aeroplane*) –

a horizontally opposed two-cylinder
engine with the help of a whiskey
bottle and an ear trumpet

gets fitted next and Lord O'Neill
of Randalstown Park, so struck
by your exploits, offers up

his level acreage as a refuge
and launching point.
(*The engine is beautifully balanced*

*but all the same the vibration
is enormous… the nuts
dance themselves loose.*)

Hooked all your life on barter –
a glider for an aeroplane, an aeroplane
for a motorcar, England

for Ireland, Ireland
for Canada – you knew this was
the single most inflammable

exchange you'd ever risk, the lone bull
standing slack under hawthorn
at the edge of the field,

quick chatter-and-flash
from the hedgerow,
enough of a canopy of willowy light

to finally allow admittance,
and saw, as you climbed up
to your tilted seat and got

those improbable Victorian pram wheels
started, a straggle of farmhands
and scullery maids,

politely assembled, all wishing you
skywards. Once it was finished,
you ran back, over and over,

to the proof it had happened: the tracks
of her passage in the spangled grass,
and then their absence –

your footprint missing on earth for the span
of a furlong, as if a giant had lifted its boot
and then set it down.

So I was born and was small for ages
and then suddenly a cardboard box
appeared with two furry black ears
sticking out of it it made me nervous
but I was brave and gave it a bell
to play with and then out it jumped
and loved me it was my cat I called it
Morris Morrissey it matched
my mother's Morris Minor

                                        For the next bit

I was a teenager and then I grew up
I had a flat in Dublin and a boyfriend
he was a vet little bed little kitchen
little towel rack lots of little cups
and saucers and then off he went
to Africa he sent me pictures
of giraffes and of the second
tallest waterfall in the world
when he got back he wasn't my friend

                                          anymore I cried

for a week I was also at university
a bigger place than school with bigger
chairs and desks and when it finished
I found a suitcase it was red
with purple flowers it had a scarf
around the handle I put in everything
I needed socks and a jotter and snacks
and took a plane across the ocean
to Japan to visit Godzilla

                                          where it was

summer and boiling hot and the people
all kept wind chimes to make it
cooler and rode bicycles to the shops
and at the same time held up umbrellas
though it wasn't even raining
and when I met a man in a bright
white classroom the darkest parts
of our eyes turned into swirls then question
marks then hearts so we got married

                              and went hippety

hoppety splat a mountain a lake
a desert we bought a house a tiny one
at first and then a massive one a baby
knocked at the door one night
but didn't come in and then another
baby came he cried a lot
we thought he had a tummy ache
we gave him a bath in a bucket
he was just lonely

                              for his sister

to come and keep him company
but you were still floating about
in space inside your bubble egg
it had accessories a switch
for going sideways a switch
for going upside down or faster
it was a cross between a sparkly green
and a sparkly silver the moon
was very annoying and then whenever

                              we'd all been bored

on our own for long enough down
you came on a path of lightning
to finish off the family you were born
on the living room floor at three
in the morning in front of the trampoline-
sofa and I heard them say *A Girl!*
and sat up straightaway we were both
pretty and I opened out my arms
and that's it really

                              When you grow up

I'm going to be *so* busy taking you
to the house shop waiting by the play-
ground gates to bring your children
swimming I won't be any different
I'll keep your room exactly as it is
for you to visit bric-a-brac collection
on the shelf the bed your father built
the letters of your name in neon
appearing on the ceiling

                              when it's time

And these, ladies and gentlemen, are the bones
of Napoleon's horse, Marengo. Articulated thus
– tibia to fibula, scapula to humerus,
appendicular skeleton latched to the dome
of the spine and the thin ribs' hanging flaps
encasing the space of the missing heart –
he seems refashioned out of a craft kit,
a balsawood model everyhorse, perhaps.
I am looking at eyes that looked at the Emperor
is nothing, however, to this: neither a coffee pot
nor toothbrush, nor His finest pearl-grey coat
from the mausoleum; not plaster
squeezed into the shape of what's been lost
to bring it back to life as a death mask,
a punched-through backwards photograph
of itself; nor any of the things embossed
by use or touch or freer association
(loose talk, hearsay) with His shining likeness –
these very hooves trod mud at Austerlitz,
this very sacrum made final victory certain.
Moreover, put your eye to the eye socket
(one by one and gently) and observe
what changes: your straight perspective curves,
the floor on which you're standing tilts,
the room's clear atmosphere thickens
and as mirrors angled off against each other
produce an endless vaulted corridor
to somewhere else, still truer things are given:
of-all-the-Russias snow, a sky of smoke,
the bite of iron, entrails in a heap,
curled up like an outgrown foal, a man asleep
inside a horse's ruptured stomach...
That's how close Marengo stands to history –
Sphenoid, Vomer, Lacrimal, Mandible –
for however long he lasts before he crumbles,

portal, time machine, skeleton key
to what cannot be imagined. Who could resist
a ticket to the steaming blooded fields
of Europe just as the dog star fades?
Hold your breath now while I show you this.

DAS DING AN SICH

East Prussia, January 1945

a pig   two cows   a dray horse   geese
by the back door   gaggle of grandmothers
kiln-dry barns   hay until summer
gardens tucked into an orderly slumber

cutlery   stewpots   teakettles   delft
eggs in a blue bowl   buttercheesehamhockmilk
tables scrubbed clean as a wishbone
spliced hares hanging from hooks   sickle-fat

wireless   gramophone   grandfather clock
a reading lamp   a newspaper rack
dead sons like icons   on the wall   *Wehrmacht*
collars starched stiff   a sewing basket

lavender bags   June stowed between folds
in a blanket chest   bed sheets   bath towels
patchwork quilts   cupboards of petticoats
nightgowns   lace   & afterwards

such ransacked   pillows
such bayoneted   eiderdowns
a white-out of feathers   in bedrooms
hallways alleyways courtyards squares

like after-Christmas snow   or nouns
unmoored   from speech
in the blistering static   of *Grossdeutscher*
Rundfunk's   final broadcast

Up on top of Divis on a freezing Saturday
we pass the singing gates: five five-barred silver yokes

across from the café (closed for renovation),
penning nothing in but their own frustration.

They keen like washerwomen into the billowing sky.
You're talking Batman, Two-Face, Robin; you lope

ahead and circle and run back, ready to walk
for hours if we have time, free at last of school

and all the worksheets you never manage to finish
on your own. I can no longer ask my grandad

exactly how his release was managed back in April
'45: five years of his young man's life wiped out

for being a so-called Enemy of the State in wartime
(that other bout of internment no one ever mentions)

and then what? Tipped out onto the pavement like a sack
of damaged apples as the gates of Crumlin Road Gaol

clanged shut behind him? My father says he walked
to this summit the very next morning, walked

to work every day thereafter, walked to think,
walked for pleasure, walked to stretch each inch of his cell

by laying it down, over and over, on the floor
of the borderless world, so that its chipped-tile cast-iron

rectangle could disappear... We opt for the Ridge Trail,
a heathery zigzag that wraps the whole side of the hill

in its ribbon, while the Joker secedes to mummification
and the death rites of Ancient Egypt. You're a dark-haired

flurry in a hailstorm, running on sugar and bliss,
who can't tell *b* from *d* because *any* letter might just flick

its Fred Astaire hat and dance backwards across the page
if it felt like it, yet starving all the same for knowledge –

imbibing the French Revolution or species of cacti
like brawn and remembering everything.

My grandad brought his own son here from the age of four
on crippling, all-day hikes on Saturdays

(long before, as the Jesuits saw it, my father had the capacity
for resistance to anything) and told him brilliant stories:

the Battle of Stalingrad, the Defence of the Luding Bridge,
The Great Only Appear Great Because We Are on Our Knees,

Let Us Rise – until the two of them fell asleep
in Hatchet Field, clouds passing over their faces like zeppelins.

The oil rigs you fell in love with a year ago
are still moored at the shipyard's glittering edge.

Storms of gunmetal grey touch down precisely in far-off
tinkertoy villages though for now we're walking in sunshine,

welcome as any downpour after a drought, as you list
the typical contents of a sarcophagus and detail the risk

of double jeopardy in the Hall of Two Truths –
Did you bring joy? Did you find joy? –

Horus skulking hawk-eyed in the background.
For most of my father's childhood, his father must have looked

like the man in the black-and-white photograph I keep sequestered
in a notebook: a Guest of Honour in the Soviet Union, turned Italian

in the Black Sea sunshine, his hallmark Donegal suit
dramatically cut, skinny like you and even more electric,

a honey magnet (and he knew it) for secretaries, receptionists,
stray passing female fellow revolutionaries

in that dim hermetic time lock called Transport House
with its tea trolleys, telephone exchanges,

ash trays standing guard along corridors
like Russian Babushkas in apartment blocks.

We can pick out its derelict white-black-and-turquoise
(Belfast's only example of Socialist Realist architecture)

from the rest of the city centre's humdrum colours.
Do you want to ask me a question, Mummy?

(by far your favourite question) as we come up at last
by our circuitous route to the granite triangulation point

where, three months earlier, my granddad's children
and their children and their children took turns with a kitchen scoop

to launch what was left of him into the air.
He'd made himself so small in the previous months,

perhaps out of courtesy, it hadn't been hard
and I want to ask you about the gates

we're on our way back to – what wind caught where?
In what cavity? Why this particular calibre of sound

unravelling only here? Are they in harmony? Are they a choir?
Are they, in fact, the singing ticket to the afterlife

and how might we post ourselves into it, limb by limb?
What scarab? What amulet? What feather? What scale? What spell?

Because of so much colour – purples greens and blues, yellow, copper, reds –
where we least expect it, Prokúdin Gorsky's outpost villagers seem more like us
dressed up than like themselves, posing in a past bequeathed to them in snatches
rather than interrupted from the task at hand. The girls look mismatched,
overfitted, stuffed into what was left after the travelling theatre's costume box
got ransacked. Old at seven, elbows out and serious as tax inspectors,
in layered skirts so beetroot they could have been soaked in soup,
these three proffer china plates of forest berries in variegated shades –
iris, magenta, plum – which ricochet in turn as a kind of rhyme
off floral handkerchiefs, pleated aprons, buttons, blouses, cuffs
dipped in dyes we haven't seen the like of. They can't be comfortable –
or are they merely wilful, staying put on the wrong side of the century,
refusing to wear trousers? The cerise shirt on the back of the man
in the open-shaft iron mine, resting on his shovel, the barge haulers,
woodcutters and troops of riverboatmen in vests the colour of duck eggs
turn 'Volga Work Parties 1905' into a room next door we might briefly visit
where nothing would surprise us. Want to see my boots? asks a foreman,
tipping up one foot at a cocky angle. The headscarf on his wife ignites a meadow.
And if, because they're richer, living in a town, or in thrall to Queen Victoria
and her calamitous black, some people have fought back their spectral natures,

choosing instead to appear to us both looped-at-the-waist and dark, the buildings behind them haven't: whole streets rise seashell pink or powder blue out of the middle picture, ringing the radical bells of themselves for miles around. Over *Golódnaya Step*, or Starving Steppe, the weather cooperates also: this sky exactly half of what's been taken two shades brighter than lazuli with no rain cloud in sight is as good as God's promise to Ishmael for the women scything a hayfield underneath it. Tashkent, Archangel, Samarkand. Here he's stopped for a moment en route (these days his perpetual state) for a rare self-portrait: hatted, moustachioed, bespectacled, thin, Chief Photographer to the Tsar. You can tell he's already distracted by the thought of his railway-car darkroom, a gift from Nicholas himself, where the three magic filters for his new magic lantern will approximate what was there. This particular Babushka on this particular veranda on this particular evening in this particular summer is spinning a skein of wool. Tomorrow night is bath night. In the morning, she'll step out of the clothes she owns including her footcloths and into her second shirt, boil a copper of water, slosh and sluice them clean with a stick of birch, then hang them out to dry all day, like the flags of a continent's countries strung across her garden, so that afterwards, her hair de-gritted and every pore alive, not a single unwashed item touches her skin.

METEOR SHOWER

Coastguard's Tower, Ballycastle

The town has long since lost
its playground of sandy children
to baths and dragons,

Scotland has flounced in its hem
and shifted itself back
over the horizon,

Gamera's been at war
with Tokyo's would-be
monster destroyers

for hours and still your father
lets you stay – guest
among our lamps and books,

the blood of two ports
alive in our glasses –
and when it's finally

properly dark, as if
launching a bird from the bowl
of his hands or morphing

into a horse, he opens a door
to a crumbling staircase
and up we troop to the roof

together, illicit
threesome without your sister,
to watch for meteors.

At first the tilt
of the planet's axis
is answered inside us –

we angle ourselves
at a slant
(though the roof is level)

then slowly straighten.
What was here in the morning
has gone – Fair Head,

Rathlin. We've stepped out
on the deck of a ship:
the lights of the marina,

of the hill-backed streets
(glowing a decorous
orange beneath us)

the ship's own hopeless
circumference in the blacked-
out ravaging sea

of everything else. The sky's
all glower and slow –
the biggest thing

in the universe
because it *is*
the universe – and so

we look up, at last.
You laugh. As though
getting flattened

by its mineral
anvil were grace,
we can't get enough

of the curtains of clouds,
closing, opening,
and the stars in behind

shining steady as lighthouses
and yes, not once but twice
– there and then there –

dust on fire at the edge
of Earth's flaying atmosphere,
scoring its signature.

You whoop and run and lean
against both of us
and look up again.

We have set
our inadequate table
and sat down

in our whitest shirts
and the guest
has come.

1

The Geologist

The rocks on Greenland are the oldest on Earth.
This one's a fossilised algal mat; this one
contains the ridges of human teeth:
some early Palaeolithic adolescent caught
grinning at the moment of death
in a stone photograph. We manoeuvre
them down to the beach on a stretcher.
Ochres and greys and blacks
ricochet back and forth across the massif,
as denuded of white as the West of Ireland,
while the shed ice bobs in the bay
begging smaller and smaller comparisons –
lozenges dissolving visibly on the tongue;
droplets of fat on broth. *If it's life*
that controls the geological machinery
of the planet, rather than the other way round,
we are neither new, nor tragic. This came
to me one morning as I sorted out my cabin
and the hundreds of marathon runners
in my brain stopped and changed direction.

The Photographer

The world speaks to me through signs.
Tiny signs. Missable signs. The stones
in the river are speaking to me.
How many decades has this ox skull lain here?
It looks like a crime scene. A waterfall
rises as mist off the face of the rock,
missing its ending. The red earth holds up
a rainbow on its outstretched hands.
We sailed right to the edge of a glacier
in a dinghy yesterday, pushed
against it, hard, but it didn't budge
or squeal. It was the colour
of desert turquoise and implacable.
When we got back, I made a map
of my life, with holes for hideouts
between birth and death, and showed it
to my friend. In the beginning,
God put a rainbow in the sky
as a promise
that He'd never let the ocean rise again.

The Geographer

IKKE OPMÅLT says the map: unexplored.
– *What's this valley called?*
– *What would you like to call it?*
For the first few days we practise
with rifles on the pebbly beach,
though it's hardly dangerous:
polar bears are visible for miles
against the darker hillsides. Bog cotton
nods in swathes above the permafrost.
Lars and Simon buzz about the sky
in their flying dinghy, taking aerial
photographs, while we concentrate
on drilling up the planet's large intestine
and seeing what it's eaten. Ridiculously
overdressed, two musk ox trundle past.
We must sound enormous –
where before there were only kittiwakes,
the occasional seaward explosion
of an iceberg disintegrating –
but they blank us nevertheless.

The Artist

I packed Anthrax,
Megadeth, Metallica. I packed
two dozen sketchpads and sixteen
boxes of pencils. Shell's Arctic exploratory
outriders in their magenta lifejackets
can kiss my shiny metal ass.
I did not pack colours. Our foremast
resembles a crucifix. I stuck my boot
on the skull of an ox as though I'd shot it
and smiled at the camera. *Running / On our way
hiding / You will pay dying / One thousand deaths...*
I straddle the prow of the ship to sketch
whatever it is I'm looking at
and the daylight lasts and lasts.
For all the white animals – the hares,
the foxes, the wolves – I just leave
spaces on the paper where their bodies were
last time I glanced up. The rest
I filibuster in in grey or black
to stop the quiet.

The Marine Biologist

FUCK EVERYTHING BECOME A PIRATE
declares my t-shirt, but I don't mean it.
Ocean invertebrates are inconceivably lovely.
Each morning, I lower a bucket over
the side of the ship, clank it back up
on deck, then stick my hand
inside the sea's feely bag. In countless
numbers, the fjord system's summer whales
perform their languid acrobatics
within metres of the bowsprit.
Transfer even a soupçon of meltwater
to a Petri dish and, hush, the world's
most previously inaccessible ballet-
dancers are practising arabesques.
Such secretly parted curtains!
Last Friday I identified
an entirely new species of Annelid,
a male and a female, framed
and translucid under the microscope's hood:
they appeared to be having sex.

The Archaeologist

Uncover a single nick on a flint
made to sharpen it and you've nailed it:
the Paleo-Eskimo village –
which must have existed
here, where this gneiss is –
hoves into view: their Big Tent
(open to the sea); their Stone Age
playground. Laughter. Dogs. Fire.
Then nothing for three hundred
thousand years and now me, in my Ushanka.
The fact was he'd gone looking for his father.
Lower down the coast, we stood
on the deck of the ship
and watched a polar bear
attacking an outpost. Then
we went to look. It had shredded
the pages of a *Reader's Digest*.
Before we got there, its long body had lolloped
away over the rocks and, even from a distance,
had kept on flashing back at us, like Morse.

Mr Duffy Jnr,
this is the third year
in a row I've snapped up a ticket
to see *Ireland's Oldest Circus*
at the scrag-end of August
& redeemed it.

After weeks
of rain, the Loughshore Park's
a lamentation of mud & leaf mulch,
made worse by your lorries'
whitewear weight. The sea
could not unswitch

the lever
of its own bad-weather-
generating mechanism even if
we begged it to. Inside,
the Big Top's dry
& dimly lit

but for the flung-
down disc of the Ring
& the children's glittery wrists
& headgear – they bob & jerk
in the smoky dark
like anglerfish

in the abyssal
trench. Drums & cymbals
crash us all awake & *before our
very eyes* the show unravels:
arctic wolves
on chairs,

acrobats
in barely-there tights
from craggy outposts in Asia
doing loop-the-loops
on Silk-Road ropes,
Marina

Ivanovitch,
taut as an unhitched
switchblade on the trapeze, swinging
herself clear of our one
credible dimension
& surviving

Sex & sugar-rot,
Tom (if I may call you that),
are your inheritance, an endless
overhauling of this cocked,
jack-in-the-box
business,

but beauty,
which is as unlikely
a gift in our genetic makeup
as your unpractised knack
for cantering bareback
standing up –

then standing
up & skipping –
is also given, so generous
the well-wishers,
so blessèd this
house.

Two cool-eyed
Ukrainians used to ride
The Wheel of Death (the *Grand
Finale*) yet this afternoon
it's *you*! – fine-tuned,
self-trained,

free –
& lo, your uncanny
balancing abilities get tendered,
recklessly, out to us
as a final sacrifice,
the bind

we can't undo
(though we don't want to).
Wind lashes the outer awning
like the last of days,
we watch you rise
to the ceiling

in a wire-strung
cage – & then run
the length of its radius, round
& round, as the trussed
massive apparatus
rebounds

each time
from its own blind
hurtling momentum down & lifts
you through & high
& over & wide
of the lip

of what we
wish for / fear, scaredy-
cat hearts in our mouths, which is
a failure of architecture –
this cradle's, yours –
which is

a slip
in your forward flip
a trip in your footwork or wiring glitch
now you're running the outer rim
– how did that happen? –
which is

gravity's
lack of mercy –
it hasn't stopped raining,
Tom, in thirteen weeks,
& still you keep
coming.

Foiled – and not for the first time –
by a timewarp villain, who sports a monocle
and a Hitler Youth haircut, who drones
about the sky in a Flying Baron
plotting his secret green riotous tectonics,
Batman – bewildered, back-footed, bilious,
shaking that metal-wedge chin of his and drooping
in the puddle of his own dejection – Batman
changes tack, hurtles deep inside the cave of his Bat
Resources and flaps out sneakily immune
to the expanding circles of dizziness that loop
the room and everyone in it in a ship's sick tilt,
emanating from the dastardly eye piece, yes,
Batman's practised crossing the mid-line
a zillion times a day, his elbows flashing
so fast they make blurry triangles, his eyes
obediently ricocheting to their corners,
inducing an ice-cream headache, Batman's
walked over the wobbly bridge of his inner
playground all the way to the end and so what
if the children stared and pointed, so what
if it took so long the sun went down
and even the moon made fun of him
with its *oh-but-the-tedium* 'O', the next time
some malefactor buckles the floor
in front of him into jagged peaks and troughs,
laughing like a maniac, or pitches a ball
at his face he hasn't been able to catch,
or urges him, sarcastically, to get on his bike
and be free – free of the ill-set, bifurcated shackles
that pin him to himself – he'll be ready:
echolocation's the least
of his snazzily packed weapons of defence
and Batman Resurrected isn't the adversary
you'd assumed you'd be dealing with, is he, in fact

you may as well order those shipping crates
lowered now, kiss goodbye
to the twenty-four-carat diamond watches
snug in their velvet cases, the bullion bars,
and come out holding your hands up, Dr Vertigo.

THE ROPE

I have paused in the door jamb's shadow to watch you
        playing Shop or Cliff! or Café or Under-the-Sea
among the flotsam of props on our tarmacked driveway.
        All courtship. All courtesy.

At eight and six, you have discovered yourselves friends,
        at last, and this the surprise the summer
has gifted me, as if some
        penny-cum-handkerchief conjuror

had let loose a kingfisher...
        You whirl and pirouette, as in a ballet,
take decorous turns, and pay for whatever you need
        with a witch's currency:

grass cuttings, sea glass, coal, an archaeopteryx
        of glued kindling from the fire basket;
you don two invisible outsize overcoats – for love?
        for luck? – and jump with your eyes shut.

And I can almost see it thicken between you,
        your sibling-tetheredness, an umbilicus,
fattened on mornings like this as on a mother's blood,
        loose, translucent, not yet in focus,

but incipient as yeast and already strong enough
        to knock both of you off your balance
when you least expect it, some afternoon after work,
        decades hence,

one call from a far-flung city and, look,
        all variegated possibles – lovers, kids, apartments –
whiten into mist; the rope is flexing,
        tugging you close and you come, obedient

children that you are, back to this moment,
    staggering to a halt and then straightening,
grown little again inside your oversize coats and shoes
    and with sea glass still to arrange, but without me watching.

Just as the world to Al-Jazari
was a wonder of *tawhid,*
all visible things

the über-florid signature of God,
so is his book
a wonder of understanding

of what can be borne up
and what will topple
given gravity, air pressure,

time, which is itself encased
in stunning script: Baikal
poured into a single

shell or glass receptacle.
Inventor of such leaps
in engineering

as the camshaft, crankshaft,
throttling valve,
the calibration of orifices

and the balancing
of static wheels – theophanies
that awed all Anatolia,

upon which our modernday
buoyancy depends –
he was also fanciful, elaborate,

absurd, who made water
issue from the fountainhead
in the shape of a shield

or *like a lily-of-the-valley.*
Flick open his pages
and listen to the clicking

of dismantled
humanoid automata
reconstructing themselves

from the bottom
up, then stepping back
from the task accomplished:

a towel proffered, a wine cup
filled, the victim
of phlebotomy distracted.

Close over the flyleaf
and watch what fades:
enamel the colour

of a peacock feather,
roundels, falcons,
anklets, diadems, bells –

fripperies
of fine technology
he stacked in Saladin's

palace workshop
solely for themselves –
which is like waking slowly

of your own accord,
the dream world oddly
tilted at your feet

for ages, for a year,
until it almost vanishes,
leaving the ghosted

impress of its ardour
still folded
in the bedclothes.

NOTES

THE MILLIHELEN. A *millihelen* is a fanciful unit of measurement meaning the amount of physical beauty required to launch a single ship. This poem describes the Titanic's successful launch into the waters of Belfast Lough in 1911.

AT THE MOSCOW STATE CIRCUS. This poem opens with the first line of 'High Talk' by W. B. Yeats.

RECEIVING THE DEAD. When Guglielmo Marconi invented the radio in 1898, he was convinced that this new technology was the perfect medium for picking up the voices of the dead. Thomas Edison and Nikola Tesla were two other famous believers in Electronic Voice Phenomena (EVP).

AT THE BALANCING LAKES. Dougal and Zebedee are two characters from the BBC children's programme *The Magic Roundabout* (1965–1977).

PERFUME. The second part of this poem draws on Patrick Süskind's novel *Perfume: The Story of a Murderer* (1985).

THE MAYFLY. In 1910, Lilian Bland, who lived in Carnmoney, County Antrim, became the first woman in the world to design, build and fly her own aeroplane.

ARTICULATION. Napoleon's horse, Marengo, was captured as a victory trophy during the Battle of Waterloo and taken to England, where he later died. His reconstructed skeleton is currently on show at the National Army Museum, Chelsea. 'I am looking at eyes that looked at the Emperor' is a quotation from *Camera Lucida: Reflections on Photography* (1980) by Roland Barthes.

WHITELESSNESS. This poem is inspired by the documentary *Expedition to the End of the World* by Daniel Dencik, first released in Denmark in 2013.

FROM *THE BOOK OF KNOWLEDGE OF INGENIOUS MECHANICAL DEVICES*. *The Book of Knowledge of Ingenious Mechanical Devices* (1206) is an early engineering masterpiece written by Ismail al-Jazari in eastern Anatolia. *Tawhid* is an Arabic word meaning the oneness of God. The lines in italics are taken from *The Book of Ingenious Devices* (850), a source of inspiration for the later text.

ACKNOWLEDGEMENTS

Thanks are due to the editors of the following publications in which some of these poems, or versions of them, have previously appeared:

Eavan Boland: Inside History (Arlen House, 2017), *Female Lines: New Writing by Women from Northern Ireland* (New Island Books, 2017), *Hwaet! 20 Years of the Ledbury Poetry Festival* (Bloodaxe, 2016), *The Mechanics' Institute Review*, *Ploughshares*, *Poetry*, *Poetry Ireland Review*, *PN Review*, *Southword*, *Subtropics* and *The Well Review*.

'Collier' was commissioned by the Durham Book Festival in 2015 as part of the Festival Laureateship. 'At the Moscow State Circus' was commissioned by Vona Groarke for a W.B. Yeats Special Issue of *Poetry Ireland Review*.